From:

Washington, District of Columbia

To:

HABANA VILLAGE

A Memoir

EDUARDO BARADA

Copyright © 2019 Eduardo Barada
All rights reserved.

Partial or total reproduction of this text is strictly prohibited.
The historical fragments included in this memoir are public domain.

ACKNOWLEDGEMENTS

I am grateful for everyone who participated in this cultural movement. In particular, I'm thankful for my friends, clients who became intimately connected with me and Habana Village and to those who also found friendships at Habana Village that remain to this day. I congratulate all the couples that found love and marriage within the context of Habana Village's art and folklore, a spiritual place thriving with culture and fostering relationships.

I give special thanks to all the businessmen who have adopted my model of cultural inclusion using music, salsa, and Cuban mojitos in the bars and restaurants of this city and other cities around the world.

I also express gratitude for the many celebrities who passed by Habana Village, enriching human relationships with their artistic, musical and literary activities.

I am deeply indebted to my friends who shared their lives with me during this important period. They were sources of motivation and support through this collective movement, and their names are forever engraved in my memory.

I would like to especially mention my colleague Cristina King, whose partnership in thought was invaluable to the success of Habana Village. Humbly stated, Cristina's participation facilitated the integration of musical artists into the cultural scene, allowing Habana Village to blossom and flourish. Our work together was genuine – me, the strategist, and Cristina, the creator of the Latin artistic line. There was much spiritual hunger at the time, abundant work to be done, and with focus, mutual support and the profound and respectful connection that bound me and Cristina, we reached our goals. My gratitude for Cristina is deep; I owe Habana Village's success to her.

I am grateful for my dear friend Emily Rose who participated constantly with a joyful presence and dynamism in Habana Village with a multifaceted personality as an artist, filmmaker and journalist.

I would also like to extend thanks to my friend Eloy Hernandez who consistently and generously helped me with the comings and goings of Habana Village, participating with his strong hand and calm presence; I recognize his support and good faith.

I am grateful for the blessings of Òlòdùmàrè and Olófin – God – and the spirit of my parents. I believe in continuing their legacy in this physical plane to motivate other spirits to achieve synarchy and see the positive results of our trajectory.

I want to acknowledge Martha and Gabriel Zapata, my direct mentors, as well as Marina Felix. And a special thank you with my absolute gratitude extends to the merchants and friends of the vanguard generation: Roberto Alvarez, creator of Café Atlántico, Guido Gerometa, Manolo Sollozo with his restaurant Rincón Español, and a special thanks to Francisco and Lucy Hernández, owners of the restaurant El Tazumal, and to their secretary Irma Campos.

Finally, I'm tremendously grateful for my partners in writing. Adriana Salazar and Rosario Gutiérrez were my first collaborators. Laura Trebs furthered the work by dedicating precious time to editing and translating, and Ofunshi Oba Koso, Babalawo/Shaman, traditional healer and spiritual diviner, guided and oversaw the direction of this book with his wisdom and collaborated with his extensive knowledge of the Yoruba religious tradition.

CONTENTS

INTRODUCTION	7
ONE CITY, WASHINGTON, D.C.	9
HABANA VILLAGE	13
THE OPENING	16
THE CLIENTS	18
THE INTERIOR	21
THE ELEMENTS: DANCE, MOJITOS AND MUSIC	24
MULTICULTURALISM, IMPARTIALITY AND FRIENDSHIP	30
THE RULE OF OSHA OR SANTERIA	36
FIRE AND REVIVAL	39
HABANA VILLAGE ENDURES	43

Habana Village

It was that kind of sky
That glows violet just before sunset
And bathes the world in Cuban night club splendor
With cicadas tuning up their singing thoraxes
And dark-eyed women patting themselves with hastily-grabbed handkerchiefs
While waiting for the Tango Man to offer the next dance.

Exotic nameless drinks are being poured
By the legless man behind the bar
While anonymous men from high in the Andes
Look over their shoulders with sun-toasted squinting
eyes at pink leggy farm girls
Laughing in love with proud young paper warriors
Who are discovering that women sweat,
Under winking lights with Lenin scowling from behind the fan
And dishes clanking in the kitchen below.

It is a world of windowless back rooms
Unencumbered by sunlight
Fueled by primal secretion from moving bodies
Tracing the sign for infinity on the painted floor.

We have discovered the perpetual rotation
In a world that is post-everything,
The ancient rhythms live on.

Poem written by a wonderful friend of Habana Village
July 21, 1995

INTRODUCTION

Much of the fascination of Habana Village was due to Barada himself and the environment he knew how to create. Having a relatively small room and without any particular feature, he managed to give the site a peculiar mystique. Beyond his classic cigar and his bald head, which gives him an unmistakable air, Barada is an undoubtedly interesting personality . . . Coming from a country where private enterprise did not exist, he became an example of a successful entrepreneur without asking for a single dollar from the government and without state contracts.

El Tiempo Latino, December 1, 1995

It was 1991, and we were suffering. Poverty and discrimination, social injustice, inequality and lack of access to public services plagued the Latin community.

That summer, while walking on Columbia Road, surrounded by the bustle of cars and buses, feeling the heat of the sun on my skin, I entered a passage full of light that transported me from Washington, D.C. to Cuba. As a Babalawo, a shaman and messenger, I felt great emotion visualizing a firm wish to establish a connection to integrate the Latin residents with the population of Washington, D.C. At that moment of enlightenment, I knew I had to create a cultural center called Habana Village. It would be situated in the Adams Morgan neighborhood with the mission to unify, foster communication and integrate the Latin community.

To achieve this objective, Habana Village would pioneer an Integral Cultural Revolution of Art and Folklore, including cultural activities to enrich the spirit and Cuban music and dance to intertwine hands and hearts.

With the establishment of Habana Village in 1992, I realized a dream. The creation of Habana Village propelled the Latin community forward into an atmosphere of inclusion and harmony; its existence activated a grassroots cultural revolution in Washington, D.C. How was it done? By employing patience, determination and spirituality. This memoir is a testimony of that accomplishment, thanks to the support and collective participation of my family, clients and friends, a narration of how it happened and the subsequent fire that proved Habana Village's endurance.

ONE CITY, WASHINGTON, D.C.

Habana Village's existence deserves a notch on the timeline of Washington, D.C.'s history; just as much as the year in which George Washington was elected president (1789) is significant in order to understand major shifts in the community and culture of the area, so too was the creation of Habana Village. The locale's innovative inclusivity cultivated a culture of diversity that began to challenge and erase the boundaries between races, skin-colors, languages and social classes.

Since its origins, the geographic area of Washington, D.C., was a very special place. The first people who populated the area were known as the Anacostians, and they used peace and integration as strategic mechanisms with area native groups to expand their commercial zone to the northeast of what is today known as the United States of America.

Creativity continued to be a theme through the city's history; at the beginning of the twentieth century there was a universal movement to celebrate achievements in art, architecture and inventions. In Washington, D.C., there was great social, economic and cultural expansion.

In 1920, women were granted the right to vote. During the rest of this decade the residents of Washington, D.C., fought to promote civic and cultural attitudes creating several civil associations favoring human rights. Also, several museums, art galleries, theaters, concert halls and the Lincoln Monument were created.

In 1947, Jackie Robinson broke the racial barrier by entering the baseball major leagues, and, in 1949, he won the most valuable player award in the National League.

Washington, D.C., was growing slowly during the 1950s, and its ethnic population and socioeconomic status was as changeable as a kaleidoscope.

Intense political activity permeated the 1960s. In Washington, D.C., the Vietnam War sparked conflicts and protests among citizens who disagreed with the war.

In 1961, John F. Kennedy became the youngest president of the United States, and during his inaugural address he motivated the citizens to act on behalf of the country. His wife, first lady Jaqueline Bouvier Kennedy, strongly influenced the expansion of the arts and the historic preservation of Washington, D.C. She started the movement with the restoration of the White House, and thanks to her advocacy, in 1963, President Kennedy created the President's Advisory Council on the Arts. During that time, Kennedy also presented the Civil Rights Bill to Congress.

Reverend Martin Luther King, since he started his pastoral career, had a leadership role in promoting civil rights for African Americans with a nonviolent approach. In 1963, during the March on Washington, he gave his speech "I have a dream". King protested the Vietnam War and poverty. In 1964, he received the Nobel Peace Prize. His assassination in 1968 motivated race riots in several cities including Washington, D.C.

The Vietnam War ended in the mid-1970s, however, most of the population was skeptical due to the political happenings of the time. Simultaneously, minorities were fighting for equality. The pressure of these groups unchained a reaction of opposition and hostility.

The 1980s brought transformation to Washington, D.C., as construction of apartment buildings, condominiums, commercial buildings and restaurants revitalized neighborhoods.

Despite the economic boom fostered by the growing urban development, the socioeconomic and ethnic inequalities were evident in the different areas of Washington, D.C., during the 1990s. Employment for minorities was scarce, and competition for the limited opportunities created an environment full of tension and hostility between select groups.

In 1991, the year before Habana Village opened its doors, Washington, D.C.'s Latin community suffered social injustice, poverty, inequality, discrimination and lack of access to public services. Daily, Latin people faced increasing conflicts, including difficulty renting houses, and abuse from select landlords who were renting units in terrible conditions. Social marginalization created impenetrable barriers for those wishing to open bank accounts and access loans. Additionally, there was no support to develop small businesses. The segregated environment within the Latin community, impunity of higher classes, and social marginalization related to ethnicity as well as social injustice contributed to disharmony between minority communities and the authorities.

The tension culminated with the massive Mount Pleasant Riots that began on May 5, 1991, when a female police officer shot an unarmed man – fear began to spread among the people as they watched the man bleed out on Mount Pleasant Street. That day news of violence spread within seconds and people started arriving, coming together, and the authorities requested back up. Piercing sirens were loud as the police arrived with several cars and a bus – they had orders to arrest and take every protester to jail. The crowd felt attacked by the police, and individuals started to defend themselves, sticks and rocks turning into weapons. The youth were running around the streets, smashing small business' doors and windows. The Latin residents, raged and tired of injustice, mobilized against police violence. Local authorities and the police were shocked by the sudden riot that broke out in D.C.'s Mount Pleasant neighborhood that afternoon. The community was in a state of emergency. Curfews were instilled the following night, and fearful of arrest, the crowds dispersed with most people returning to their homes. Violence and pillage ceased, and calm returned to the neighborhood. However, discontentment, fear and segregation remained heavy, burdening the atmosphere.

Days and nights passed as D.C. hovered under a blanket of violence that was becoming more acute, each day seeing increasing crime and people suffering with insecurity and bewilderment. The lack of spirituality in the people was the living reality in Washington, D.C., at that time, and communities felt abandoned by recent events. The double moral in the religious and political institutions became evident. As a Babalawo, a shaman, and as a witness, my spiritual alarm was triggered, and my living spirit became aware as I questioned myself about the role I was playing in the course of D.C.'s experiences; my living spirit knew I had to find the perfect code to silence this catastrophic alarm.

It was then, only months after the Mount Pleasant Riots, during the summer of 1991 that the idea of Habana Village occurred to me in a vision; the desire was intense to create a space allowing Washington, D.C.'s Latin residents to integrate. I knew cultural activities, art, music and dance would be included and would foster physical, emotional and spiritual connection. The idea for Habana Village was born – while the concept and purpose was very clear, the how and where of its implementation remained a mystery.

HABANA VILLAGE

If postmodernism is represented by the subsistence of "amputated" symbols of their original contexts and mixed in a confused but vital environment capable of giving them a new meaning – even if one does not know which one –, Habana Village was undoubtedly a monument to postmodernism.

El Tiempo Latino, December 1, 1995

Implementing the cultural center proved to be difficult; restrictions and obstacles slowed me from realizing my plan, but I continued searching with persistence for the perfect place to build Habana Village.

I knew Habana Village would be located in northwest Washington, D.C., in Adams Morgan neighborhood. This was my community, and it was full of movement and color. Strolling down 18th Street you could find a variety of flavorful restaurants lined one next to the other, the aromas of international cuisine inviting you in to savor dishes from Ethiopia, Jamaica, France, El Salvador, America, Mexico, Spain and Italy. Columbia Road was another popular street with its length connecting several neighborhoods of the city. Pedestrian and vehicular activity was prominent along the commercial area full of shops and restaurants.

In 1990, Adams Morgan was considered the most multiculturally-populated area of the city, with 30 percent of the community Anglo-American, 30 percent African American and 30 percent Latin. It was also the most densely populated neighborhood of African, Asian and Indonesian immigrants. Adams Morgan lacked a cultural center to integrate the Latin groups living in the area; it had no collective reference, it had no place where Latins could find shelter.

The path to give Habana Village roots was full of barriers, but Òlòdùmàrè and Elegbara – owner of paths and destiny – mobilized their energy to protect me. One day when I was feeling defeated by the unfruitful search, Benny, the owner of a restaurant on 18th street came to visit.

"Eduardo," he told me, "there's an empty space on the second floor of El Tazumal restaurant – you should talk to the owners and ask them to rent it to you."

I looked at him skeptically and jokingly replied, "No, Benny, you go and ask them, and let me know."

The next day, Benny came to tell me, "Eduardo, this is the telephone number for Lucy and her husband so that you can call them. They are willing to rent you the place."

The opportunity had arrived after several months of exploring, thanks to my protectors Elegbara and Òlòdùmàrè, and to Benny, their messenger. The owners of "El Tazumal" agreed to rent me the space on the second floor of their restaurant. Habana Village grew solid roots, and our address would be 2400 18th St. NW, Washington, D.C.

The second floor of the building had been empty for a long time and required cleaning and remodeling. The space was rectangular, and, with the help of friends, I refurbished it to mimic the style of cultural centers in Cuba: simple aesthetics with white walls, wooden shelves, and with traces of the spiritual resonance of my religion, the Rules of Osha, popularly known as Santeria. Very close to the entrance I placed my protector Elegbara, which represents the Holy Child of Atocha, the one that opens or closes the path of life, gives prosperity, happiness, luck or disgrace.

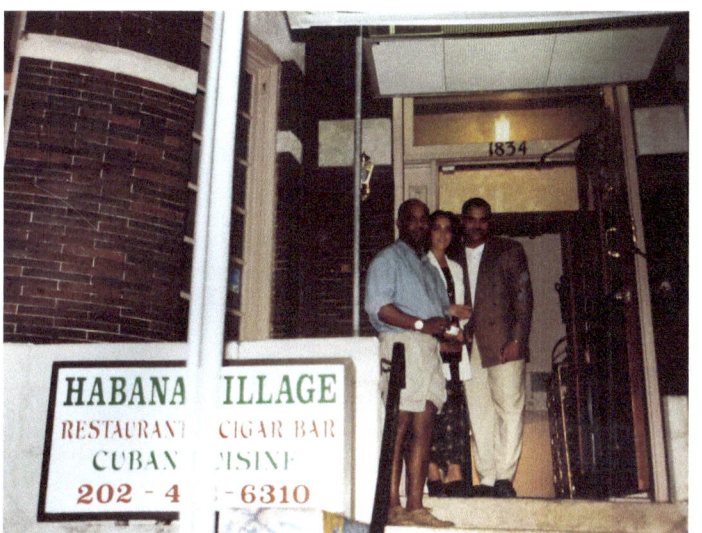
Entrance to Habana Village. Aristire (security chief), Ana and Eduardo.

THE OPENING

Securing licenses and permits before operating Habana Village was tedious. I looked at each passing day with impatience and difficulty; working and waiting was all I could do. The year 1991 was coming to a close as I labored intensively for several weeks to bring Habana Village's interior to life and prepare for the great opening.

Soon after the New Years, everything was finally ready, and with a great deal of emotion I finally chose Saturday, February 14, 1992, to formally open the doors of Habana Village, the same day Latin American countries celebrate love and friendship.

On inauguration day, the bar was stocked. The aroma of mint and lime from the mojitos swirling with tendrils of tobacco smoke announced the opening of Habana Village, and notes of Cuban music floated down the stairs, dispersing throughout 18th street. We didn't have flyers or any sort of formal propaganda; our opening was spread by word-of-mouth and with rhythm around the neighborhood, news extending to the entire city and reaching beyond to neighboring states

My friends were the first ones to arrive, and they just happened to bring others looking to celebrate the day of love and friendship at a party filled with mojitos and Cuban rhythms. That day Habana Village was full, and it continued to be like that every single day as clients entered and later found they couldn't leave, mesmerized but the locale's energy.

As a courtesy and as an integrative and unifying symbol, every guest who shared opening night with us received a lifetime membership, giving them the privilege of entering Habana Village for free forever, even during special events.

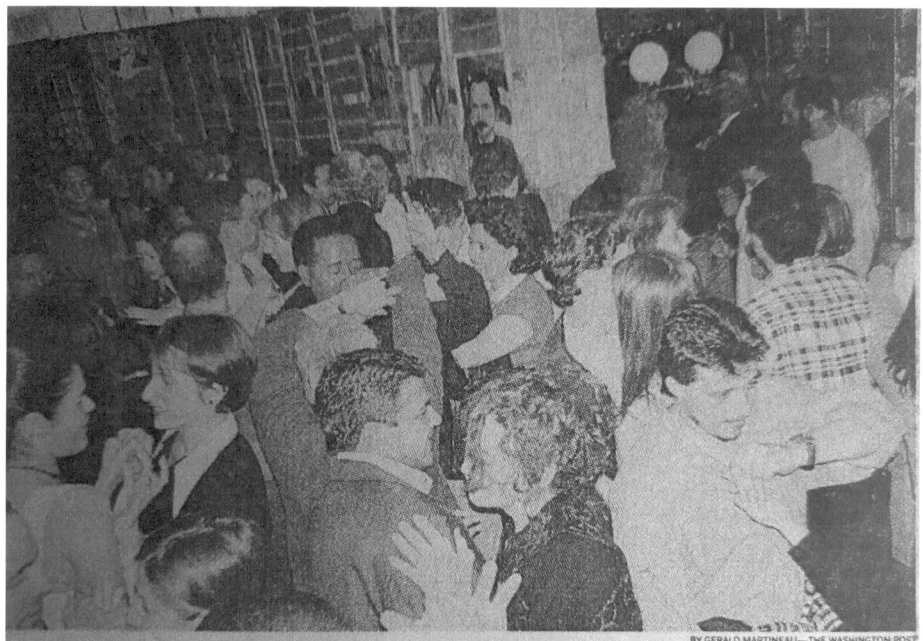

The Opening

THE CLIENTS

The first clients were my beautiful friends, all in favor of celebrating culture and mutual respect with the rhythm of Habana Village. Their names were: Emily, René, Julia, Ramberto, Claudia, Rosario, Willy, Isabel, Pedro, Janet, Juan, Ricardo, Irma, Daniel, Ana, Eric, Nicole, Alex, Susana, Hugo, Peter, Rosa, Abram, Alice, Benny, Ann, Miguel, Mario, Jorge, Isabel, Marisa, Luis, Gwendell, Larry, Sally, Reynol, Nando, Daniel, Richardson, Luciano, Maino, Ernesto, Sahara, Miguel Angel, María Cristina, Caban, Rea, Fred, Dimitri, Serrano, Marina, Dona, Susana, Ernesto William, Rigores, Aury, Cristian, Luis Alberto, Cristo, Wagner, Cynthia, Ricardo, Pepe, Rada, Lorga, Manuel, Nadia, Eladio, Gustavo, Roberto, Margarita, Hugo, Viki, José, Rhonda, Raúl, Angie, Roberto, Gutierrez, Teresa, Patrick, Mary, Ramón, Alicia, Harriet, Pat, Carmen, Jorge, Sharon, Menéndez, Francis, Susan, Sandra, Mireya, Roberto, Ellen, Luis, Lillian, Reiza, Leo, María, Angel, Michelle, Ramón, Miguel, Angel, Janet, Sussy, Antonio, Gabriel, Silvia, Bruno and many more.

When people spread the word about Habana Village's opening, the public rushed in, following the notes of Cuban music and the smell of mint and lime. They climbed to the second floor, curious to find a full room of people immersed in dancing, and they integrated immediately into the unique experience of fraternity, inclusion, and open communication where all clients interacted respectfully with each other, accepting and embracing the rhythm of Cuban music.

Some clients found love at Habana Village, rhythm and dance connecting souls. One example is Janet who met her German husband there, and just recently they celebrated 25 years of marriage. Janet's family history at Habana Village doesn't stop there. She was a regular who came every day after work as an academic with a PhD. She would dance all night, gracing the locale with her energy and rhythm. One day a woman approached the entrance asking for Janet, explaining she was her mother.

"Janet tells me she comes here every day," she said, "so I came by to see what my daughter does here."

Habana Village's spirituality and vibe fascinated Janet's mother, and after that particular night, she returned to Habana Village every day sharing the music, dance and mojitos with her daughter.

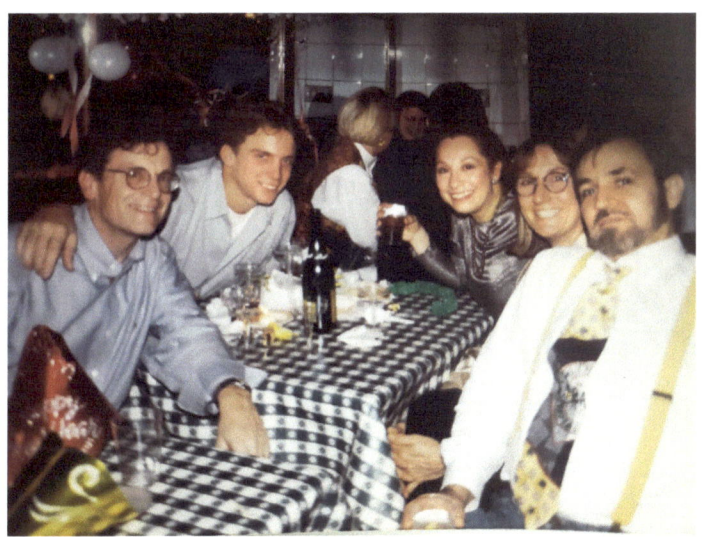

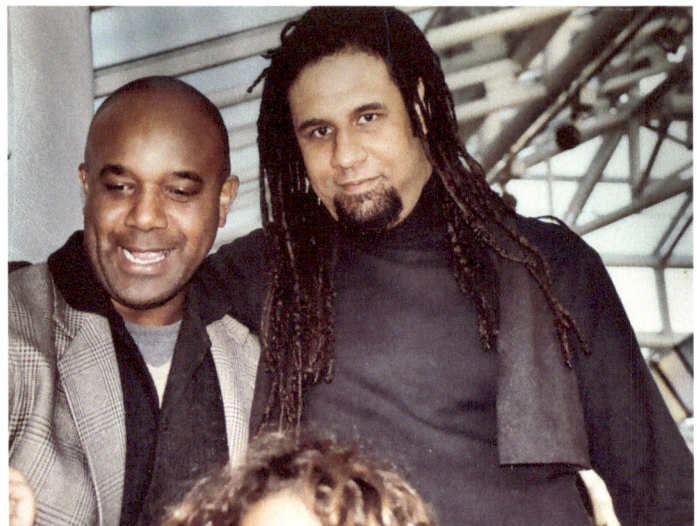
Eduardo and Raynol

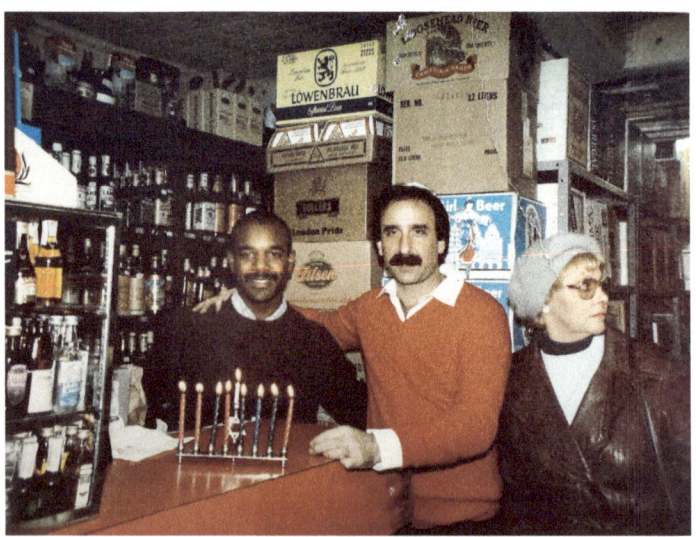
Eduardo Barada and Steve Felman.
A good friend who always supported Habana Village.

THE INTERIOR

After walking through Habana Village's wooden front door and climbing the carpeted stairs to the building's second floor, the entire room was visible, including the dance floor and the bar to the right of the entrance. The entrance's location was strategic as it provided total visibility, allowing visitors to witness the dancing in a blink of an eye, the flow of people and the crowd's movements.

The dancefloor covered much of the space, allowing a vast canvas for people to paint a lively and multicolor landscape with their bodies as they danced. The bar countertop offered free food for people to enjoy – yellow rice, empanadas and cold snacks. Every day the menu changed.

Visible from the bar was an art gallery where artists complemented a plural and multifaceted scene with their lives and stories, building a landscape of multicultural and polyethnic integration of art and folklore.

The white walls that started empty soon became covered with photographs of my clients taken by my friend Daniel. Also hanging on the wall was a portrait made for me by my friend Emily Rose. Habana Village's guests started to print their names and dates of visit on the wall as a way of expressing their joy. One time, an image appeared of a heart with an arrow and the name of a loved one, and that figure was replicated many times by others. Those simple graffiti expressions evolved into verses, poems and song fragments covering the entirety of the walls. The graffiti, like a living body, expanded from floor to ceiling, the etching allowing each guest to feel like they belonged with Habana Village. The abstract walls spoke of harmonization, flags from every country and Afro-Cuban artwork hung as decoration.

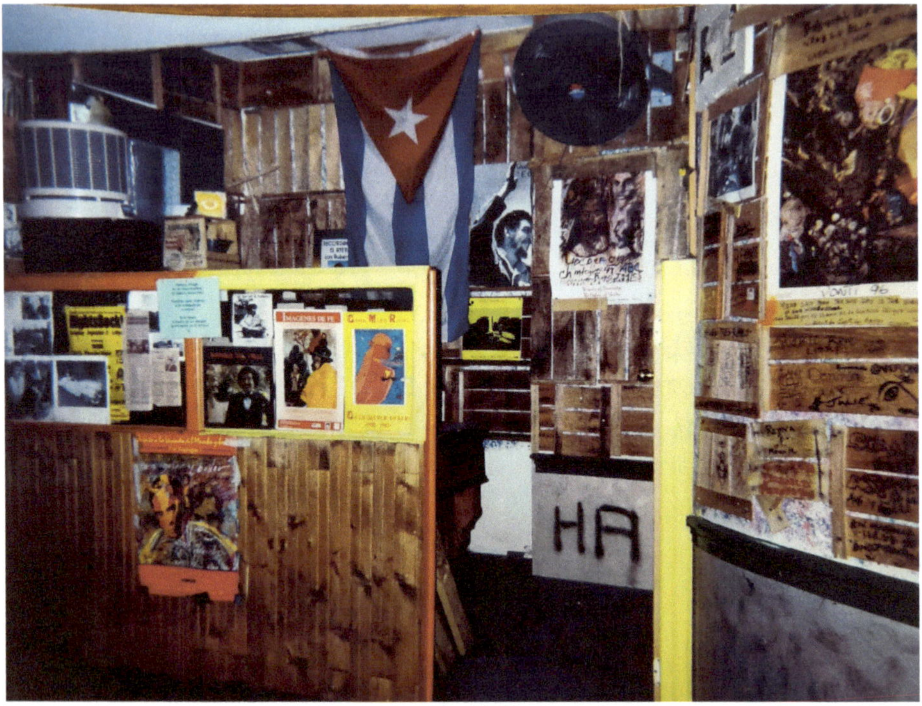

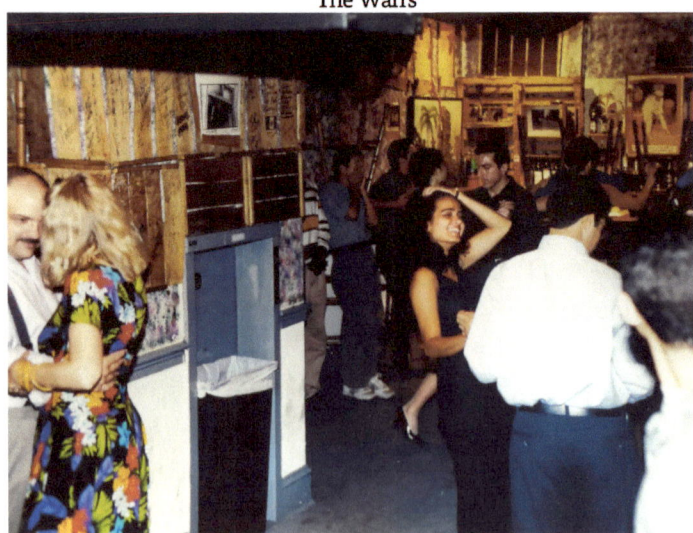

The Walls

Tropical night at HabanaVIllage. Tobacco, Rum and Mojito.

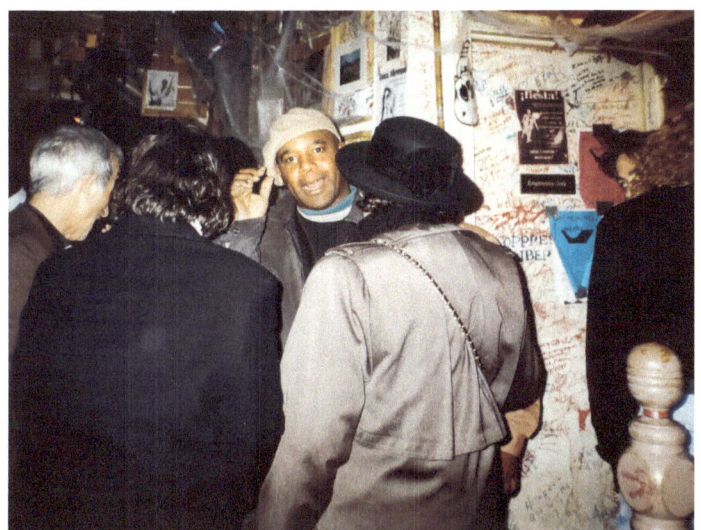
Eduardo Barada. Friends forever at Habana Village

THE ELEMENTS: DANCE, MOJITOS AND MUSIC

Art and folklore were more important than politics, and on that axis revolved the magic world of the place, where Barada knew how to offer a bit of everything but without betraying the Afro-Cuban heritage, which in that climate could easily become a universal concept.

El Tiempo Latino, December 1, 1995

DANCE

Dance, Cuban music and mojitos enhanced the spiritual effect of collective communication of Habana Village's Art and Folklore.

Even though Habana Village was never presented as a disco club, guests were drawn to move to the rhythm of the music, following the Cuban tradition and exercising their freedom of expression through dance. By nature, dancing also facilitated connections.

At first, non-Latin clients felt a bit restrained when they saw couples masterfully dancing the Cuban rhythms of salsa, mambo and cha-cha-chá. Some had never before heard or seen anyone dancing to Cuban music – they were perplexed by the Latin dancers and the sharp turns that made their partners appear as if they were floating on the dance floor.

I immediately organized dance workshops at Habana Village so everybody could integrate. We offered salsa and flamenco classes on Wednesdays and Fridays and tango classes on Saturdays. The instructors – some of them American like Gerry, Leon and Rafael, or Miguel, who was Panamanian, Carolina from Colombia, Julia from Spain and Ramberto from Dominican Republic – were multicultural, teaching the different Cuban rhythms with simplicity and sensitivity, initiating many non-Latins into Latin dancing, imparting confidence in every new step. Each instructor's style of dance reflected their Latin American and Spanish origins, and they were experts at Cuban rhythms.

The dance classes, along with dancing Latin clients who turned into volunteer trainers, helped non-Latin participants developed the ability to feel and move to the music. The interaction between clients during these gatherings facilitated the birth of friendships that continue today.

MUSIC

At Habana Village a flow of Cuban musical notes possessed a power to connect and embrace the group, intensifying a spiritual communication.

The swing of Benny Moré's song *Bonito and Sabroso* would resonate down the narrow wooden stairwell, catching the attention of people strolling 18th street – guests would stop by the door, peer up the entryway and curiously begin climbing the stairs. Some were indecisive, shyly approaching the second floor as others would rush to the dance floor. Guests might linger by the bar, relaxed and sipping their mint and lime-scented mojitos, and others would feel drawn to dancing by simply hearing the rhythm of Cuban music.

They were welcomed by the notes of those who represented Cuban music: Paquito D'Rivera's *Adagio*, Mario Bauzá's *Yo Soy el Son*

Cubano, Cachao's *A Gozar Timbero*, Trio Matamoros' *Son de la Loma*, Septeto Nacional de Ignacio Piñeiro's *El Adiós de Este Momento* and *Suavecito*, Benny Moré y Su Banda Gigante's *Qué Bueno Baila Usted*, Compay Segundo, Efraín Ferrer and Elena Burke's *Mi Son Entero*, Elíades Ochoa and Buena Vista Social Club's *El Cuarto de Tula* and many more Cuban artists.

Live musicians often blessed Habana Village with their rhythms. My dear friend Cristina King had created a program with Washington Performing Arts and started to bring Hispanic artists to Habana Village. Irakere, Los Muñequitos de Matanzas, Orquesta de la Luz, Los Van Van and El Grupo Percucionista de Mujeres Cubanas con Ibbo Okun are just a sample of artists who filled the locale with their presence and vibrations.

Music was foundational to Habana Village, just as music's role in the Latin American culture is the groundwork out of which life occurs. Regardless of country or style, music plays an integral role in every Latin American culture. Babies are exposed to rhythm and movements even before they're born by their dancing mothers. It's also infused into simple rituals like singing lullabies to invite sleep or to accompany play and meal time. Adults use music to mourn and to celebrate, during heartaches and also moments of joy, which is why hearing the beat of Cuban musicians at Habana Village was so enticing. Clients came from all walks of life, and the unifying factor, the magnet, drawing them together was the music.

CUBAN MOJITOS

Our Cuban mojitos made history as its prevalence on drink menus across Washington, D.C., and the bars of many cities, nationally and internationally, started to increase once its discovery at Habana Village. It's one of the most famous cocktails in the world now for its simplicity and flavor. A simple and artisanal drink with impactful flavor, the mojito is made with freshly squeezed lime juice mixed with mint leaves, sugar, rum and sparkling water.

The mojito drink was actually created initially to be a medicine. When the English Capitan Sir Francis Drake docked in La Havana during one of his expeditions, with his crew sick with scurvy, Cuban doctors prepared them a syrup with aguardiente, lime, sugar and mint and achieved excellent results. The syrup with such great flavor was called The Drake, which over time changed its name to mojito.

Habana Village Cuban Mojito Recipe

2 teaspoons sugar
2 sprigs of mint
½ lime, cut in pieces
Sparkling water
1.5 ounces rum
4 ice cubes

Preparation: Add sugar, sliced lime and mint to a small glass. Blend the ingredients using a mortar. Add the ice and rum. Top with sparkling water as needed. Cheers!

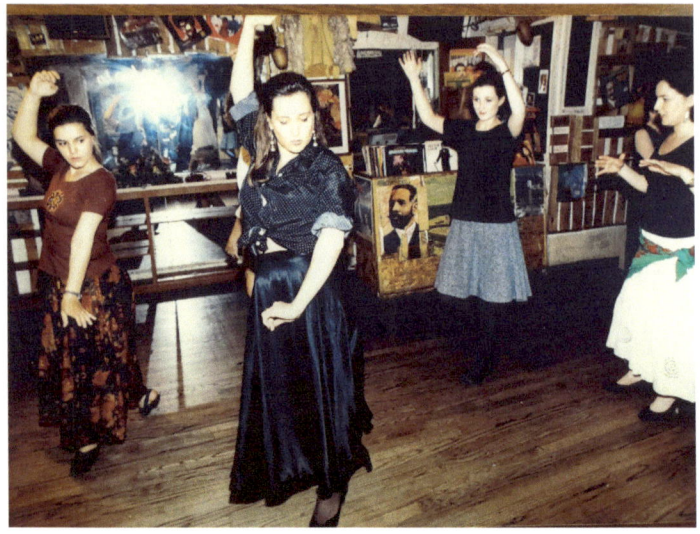

Julia Aymerich Flamenco Professor at Habana Village with her students
Elena, Ruth, Mila, Susana and Donna

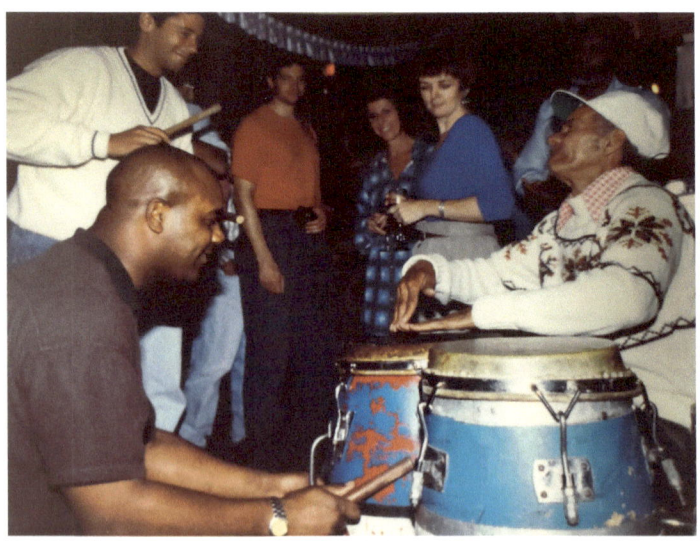

Maestro Francisco Rigore, symbol of Cuban art and folklore

Afro-Cuban group "Muñequitos de Matanza"

MULTICULTURALISM, IMPARTIALITY AND FRIENDSHIP

The profile of Habana Village was that there was no profile: a living representation of a true multiculturalism and an "open" space where the public did not have any predominant feature. The slight anachronism of the place put it beyond fashion, time and space.

El Tiempo Latino, December 1, 1995

Habana Village's culture was plural and multiethnic; both Latin and non-Latin clients felt in absolute harmony with the location's atmosphere without even perceiving the ethnic, academic or socioeconomic differences. At Habana Village, every client was valued and precious, even the sly ones!

One night, the doorman asked me to cover a few minutes for him. While I was at the door, a man arrived and said, "Look, I'm friends with Eduardo. He told me I could come in for free, and I also have four guests."

"Are you friends with Eduardo?" I asked

"Yes," he replied.

"Do you know him well?" I probed again.

"Yes," said the man again. "Eduardo and I have been very good friends for many years."

"Well," I said, "If you are friends with Eduardo, let us honor his word and allow you and your guests in."

At that very moment while the man and his friends were still standing by the door, the doorman came back and told me, "Eduardo, you have an urgent phone call."

The man looked at me and said, "Are you Eduardo? Man, I'm so sorry!"

We shook hands, and not only did he become a regular of Habana Village, but also a friend.

Friendship, respect and courtesy greeted every guest; accomplishing its mission, everyone was treated equally at Habana Village, and the Latin community knew there was no other place like this in Washington, D.C.

Our staff represented the multiculturalism of the area. The barmen were Cuban, Chinese-Cuban, Vietnamese, Russian, Brazilian, Salvadorian, Dominican, French, English and Venezuelan; Chino, Aldo, Reynol, Fred, Dimitri, Wagner, Marina, Susan, Vicky, Ricardo and Bruno, amongst other, embraced their roles at Habana Village.

Every day at Habana Village something unique happened: guests stepped into the locale, crossing the threshold, and left their social classes hanging at the entrance like coats on hooks. We witnessed linguistic, academic and professional diversity; just as politicians would visit Habana Village to chat and integrate with the crowd, so too would laborers visiting after a physically exhausting work day to enjoy the collectivity where everyday solitude was erased by the spiritual alternative of art and folklore. Habana Village embraced everyone, including painters, employees of big corporations, congressmen, diplomats, construction workers, senators, lawyers, plumbers, bankers, artists, actors, writers, carpenters, theater directors, university professors, filmmakers, electricians, reporters, television producers, printers, employees of international organizations, among others.

Many famous personalities passed through Habana Village and were welcomed with the same respect and courtesy as was provided to the rest of the clients. These personalities, surprised by the rich atmosphere of inclusion and equality, interacted with my clients as equals. For example, painter, filmmaker and journalist Emily Rose contributed her energy to Habana Village activities and subsequently became a good friend. Barack Obama also visited Habana Village, as well as Gabriel García Márquez, *el mensajero de la paz* y Nobel Prize winner for Literature who shared and danced with the public. Referring to Habana Village, García Márquez said: "This is a real place."

Amongst other artists, we had Afro-Cuban painter Manuel Mendive, Cuban poets Pablo Armando Fernández, Pedro Sarduy and Miguel Barnet, Peruvian writer Mario Vargas Llosa, and we welcomed actors Natalia Herrera, Emilio Estévez, Edward J. Olmos, Richard Dreyfuss and Robert Duvall who all enjoyed Habana Village. Paco de Lucía, a regarded Spanish guitar player, frequented Habana Village, as well as musicians Cachao, Mario Bauza, Issac Delgado, Chucho Valdez, Mick Jagger, Dizzy Gillespie and many others. My clients had something in common with these personalities: for a moment, at Habana Village, they were as famous as them.

Just as equality was valued at Habana Village, so was diversity and individuality. Various groups of people from similar cultures began gathering at Habana Village, and to foster that conviviality, we organized weekly social gatherings to give those groups opportunities to celebrate their national identity in a unique space where everyone was invited. Monday was Russian night; Tuesday, French night; Wednesday, Brazilian night. That was the clientele of Habana Village – multinational, multicultural and multilingual.

Habana Village also focused on social justice, opening its doors to several community organizations and non-profits, sponsoring cultural events in favor of Cuban children and young people in the Latin community of Washington, D.C. We also worked with the Pan American Health Organization (PAHO) to promote education on AIDS prevention. The social gatherings were at midnight. We showed educational videos provided by PAHO followed by a question and answer session to clarify doubts and promote health in the community.

At Habana Village, besides music, dance and mojitos, clients and community members enjoyed a coexistence where everyone was equal and communication was always respectful and fun. It was a meeting place where all participants shared the joy of life in a calm and safe environment.

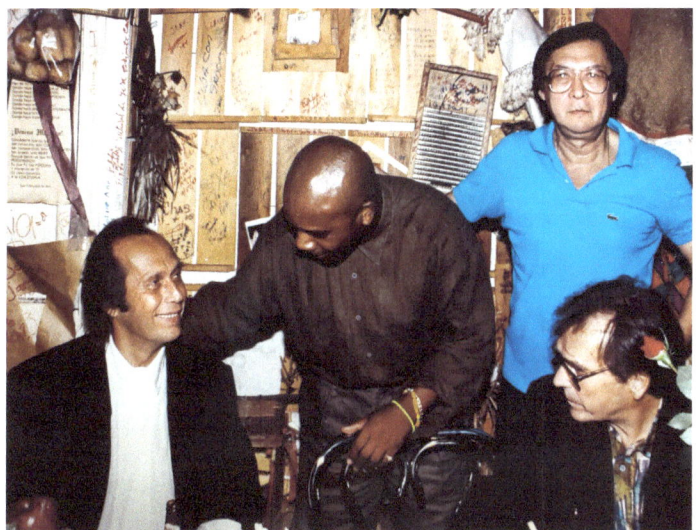

Paco de Lucía, Eduardo Barada, Aldo (Cuban Chinese, creator of the Mojito in DC at Habana Village) and Paco's manager.

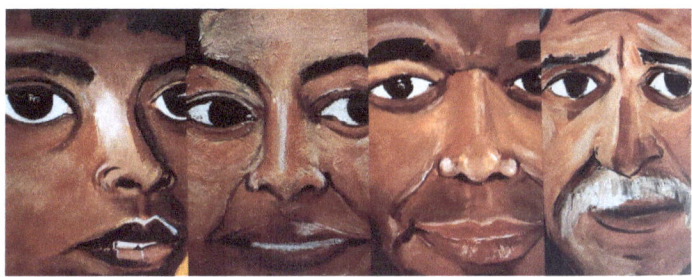

"La Mirada" painting by Emily Ross.
Niño, Rosario, Eduardo and Naul.

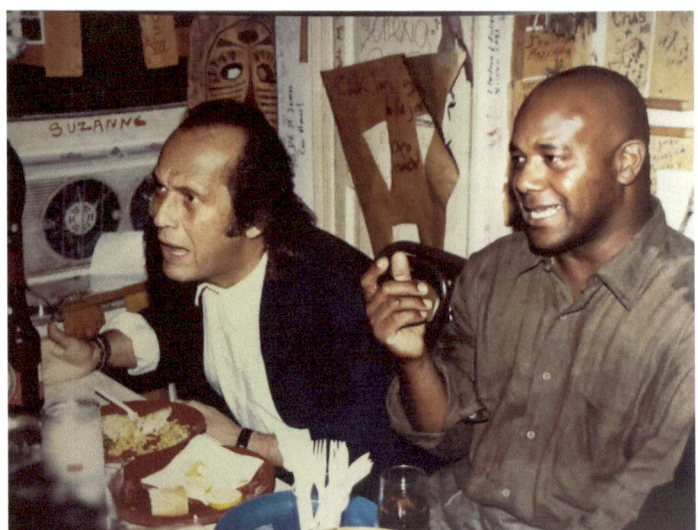
Paco de Lucía and Eduardo Barada socializing with the clients.

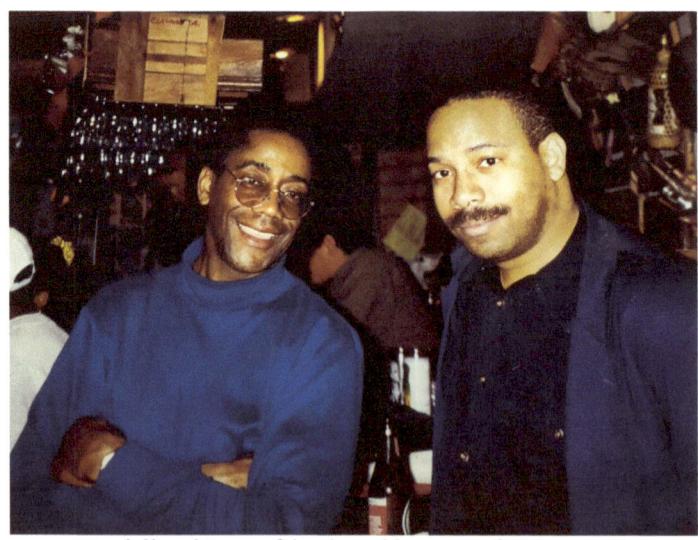
Wendell and Larry, friends and lawyers of Habana Village.

HABANA VILLAGE

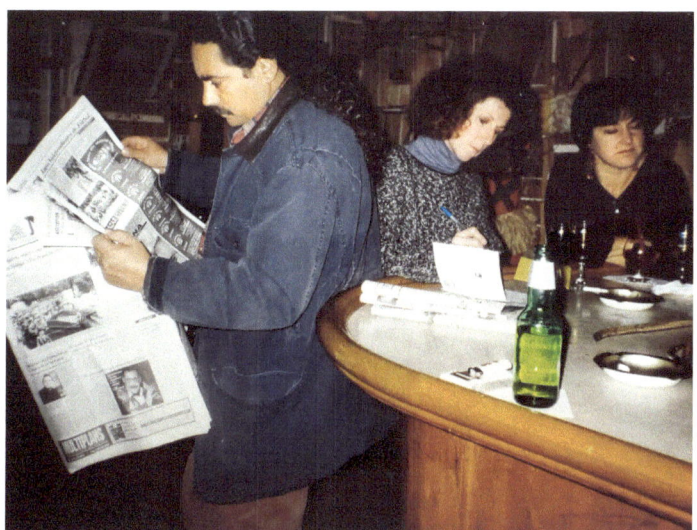

Intellect at Habana Village. Daniel and Susana.

THE RULE OF OSHA OR SANTERIA

There was only one limitation: you could not enter the place with a hat, because that is forbidden by Santeria. . . to which Habana Village is ascribed.

El Tiempo Latino, December 1, 1995

Spirituality played a substantial role in every aspect of Habana Village, from the moment I visualized Habana Village's existence and mission to the way the locale was able to draw people together and break down barriers. I owe the role of spirituality to my belief in the Rule of Osha or Santeria. This religion was born in Cuba, having been developed with both the principles of the catholic and Yoruba religions; the combination and transposition of these two religions is known as syncretism.

Santeria spread with the migration of several practitioners who left Cuba looking for better opportunities; this religious practice became popularized and internationalized in the last three decades of the twentieth century. Specifically, in 1980, the arrival of Cuban migrants famously known as "Marielitos" to the Florida coasts contributed to the establishment of the religion which continues to be visible today.

Due to the expansion of Santeria both inside and outside of Cuba, the island's government decriminalized the acclaimed religion. Cuba, New York, Miami and Washington, D.C. became great Santeria temples for its practitioners and new members. Today we have a great number of people initiated in the Rule of Osha worldwide, favoring and enriching the spirits of its practitioners.

In the inclusive principles of the Rule of Osha every person is welcome. Because of this, Habana Village attracted diversity and radiated acceptance. Every night was different as the leadership of Habana Village motivated and aroused curiosity in a spiritual life; we educated guests in the celebrations and rituals of the Afrocuban religion as they fled their own religious concepts because of the scandals and double morality that many religious and political institutions exerted. At Habana Village they discovered that the Osha accepted them with all of their taboos.

With its popularity, Habana Village was like the impulse which drove not only guests but also anthropologists, newspapers and television reports to explore further the notion of spirituality; television networks – Univision, London BBC, German TV, Spanish TV, the voice of the Americas, and Radio Martí from Cuba – came to Habana Village to record live images of art and folklore, and the cultural revolution of Habana Village expanded in response to the existing needs. Habana Village's presence and lasting spirit eventually expanded, the model replicating in several cities around the United States, Canada, Mexico and Europe.

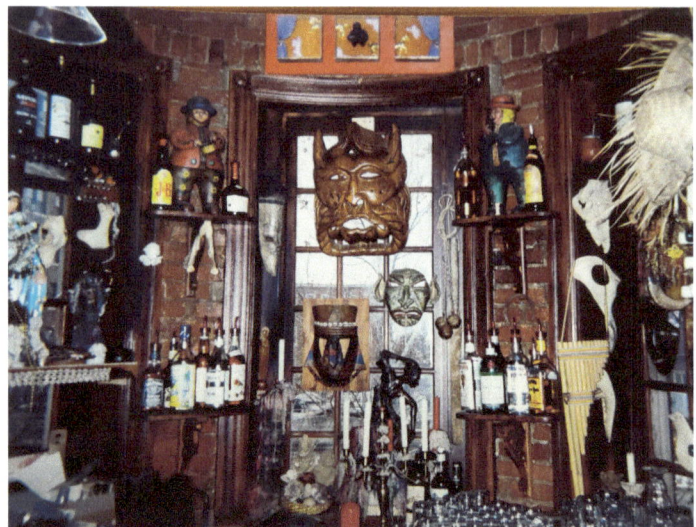

Midnight art cafe, live music, art gallery

FIRE AND REVIVAL

Havana village ceased to exist at dawn last Thursday . . . Fortunately, there were no victims, although the material damage was significant

El Tiempo Latino, December 1, 1995

By 1996 Habana Village was thriving, as were the guests who adored the atmospheres and flourished with its energy. I didn't foresee destruction, but on Friday, November 27, 1996, our lives changed. After guests had left for the night, I switched off Hanaba Village's lights and pulled the door closed, leaving everything as I usually did and headed home. It was three o'clock in the morning.

Two hours later I was woken up by the piercing ring of a telephone. It was a friend frantically reporting a fire at Habana Village and neighboring restaurant El Tazumal. My body shook with the news, and I rushed to Habana Village. I felt a deep emptiness and like a ball of barbed wire fence had sprung open inside of me, cutting into my being.

Fire trucks and police vehicles lined the streets in front of Habana Village. The smell of smoke and charred building permeated the streets and soaked the atmosphere. By the time I'd arrived, the core of El Tazumal and Habana Village was destroyed, reduced to ashes layering the floor and scraps of wood scattered on the street. The fireman had already extinguished the fire and were checking for residual embers. Within minutes, everything had disappeared; the life of Habana Village and El Tazumal had collapsed. The beautiful graffiti, the pictures, the paintings and irreplaceable music records – they were all destroyed.

That cultural movement, which started as a dream, filling the hearts of thousands of people, strengthening bonds and forming families, was extinguished with the fire.

I stood in front of my dream, in front of the ashes of what had become of a home so special to me and to every guest that visited Habana Village. The locale united differences, erased social classes and provided an environment of joy and community. Tears flooded my eyes as I saw the sign reading "Salsa Classes at Habana Village" discarded on the sidewalk in front of what was once the entrance to Habana Village.

Remembering this devastation is painful; when trying to explain the memories, still to this day words stick like claws to my throat and to my guts. The pain of losing a dream was demoralizing. The support of my wife and friends carried me through those difficult months.

THE MOVE AND REVIVAL OF HABANA VILLAGE

The community was shocked with the news, the local newspapers describing the catastrophe with precision. *El Mundo Latino*, *Washington Hispanic*, *El Tiempo Latino*, *Univision* – everyone told the story of the loss. That Friday the regulars of Habana Village gathered near the ashes, united in pain and sadness. Many had tears flooding their eyes. It was a collective loss.

That very same day several businesses in Adams Morgan neighborhood proposed hosting the Habana Village community and friends. Pepe Luján, was one of those owner and offered the space of his cafe Avignon Frères to give continuity to the cultural movement that the fire interrupted. A sound system was donated, and Habana Village's community congregated, dancing all night to Cuban music, sad but together. The loss of Habana Village had been abrupt, but despite the sadness, the followers of the art and folklore movement were there dancing.

Soon thereafter, *The Washington Post* announced that Habana Village's family was looking for a new home to continue its journey. Investors from the community gathered, proposing a backup plan to continue my project and inject Habana Village with new life. Among the several propositions, I chose the most ideal, and Habana Village entered its second stage. After a few months spent temporarily at Avignon Freres and exactly four years after Habana Village first opened, on February 14, 1996 – the day of love and friendship – we were again celebrating as we inaugurated a new and spacious premise on Columbia Street. The locale was packed tight with Habana Village's family.

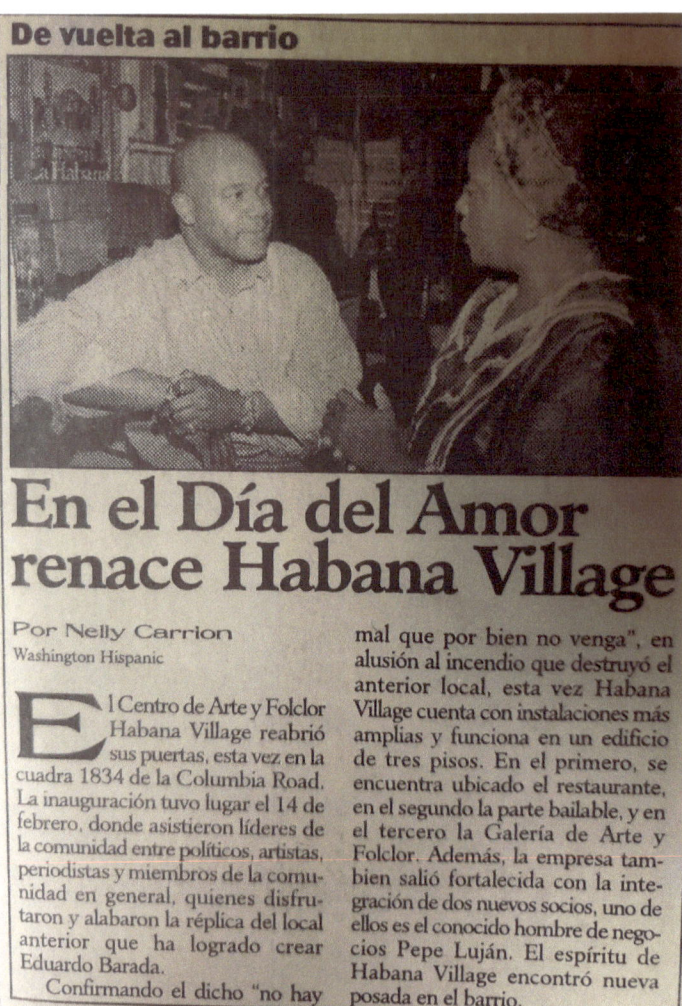

De vuelta al barrio

En el Día del Amor renace Habana Village

Por Nelly Carrion
Washington Hispanic

El Centro de Arte y Folclor Habana Village reabrió sus puertas, esta vez en la cuadra 1834 de la Columbia Road. La inauguración tuvo lugar el 14 de febrero, donde asistieron líderes de la comunidad entre políticos, artistas, periodistas y miembros de la comunidad en general, quienes disfrutaron y alabaron la réplica del local anterior que ha logrado crear Eduardo Barada.

Confirmando el dicho "no hay mal que por bien no venga", en alusión al incendio que destruyó el anterior local, esta vez Habana Village cuenta con instalaciones más amplias y funciona en un edificio de tres pisos. En el primero, se encuentra ubicado el restaurante, en el segundo la parte bailable, y en el tercero la Galería de Arte y Folclor. Además, la empresa también salió fortalecida con la integración de dos nuevos socios, uno de ellos es el conocido hombre de negocios Pepe Luján. El espíritu de Habana Village encontró nueva posada en el barrio.

Back to the neighborhood. The revival of Habana Village.

HABANA VILLAGE ENDURES

> *Today its [Habana Village] creator Eduardo Barada does not shy away from misfortune, and he is determined to rise up among the ashes like a phoenix. The history of the Habana Village has not died, it continues inviting to dance.*
>
> Carrion, *Washington Hispanic*, December 1, 1995

Infused with love and simplicity, Habana Village's energy was vibrant. The reincarnation of the free spirit became evident in the energetic flow that reached all visitors and kept everyone happy.

When I established Habana Village, my intention was to create a constellation where human joy formed a collage that was part of a living art gallery. My motivation was to assume the responsibility of being, of existing – with energy and respect for leaders – opening paths and participating with joy in society's transformation.

Before Habana Village's existence, Washington, D.C., lacked spiritual leadership and there was an overarching sense of lost spirits in search of shelter and positive change. It is vital to point out that in any society when spirituality is omitted, there are no leaders – there is only invalid work and opportunism. Our people were disoriented and in a limbo created by distrust in religious and political institutions. Habana Village's appearance was like the advent at the peak of chaos; a meeting point was achieved, delivering spiritual dynamism that fused the masses – this was the integral revolution of Habana Village. By utilizing non-violence, art and folklore, Habana Village fulfilled the role of spiritual leader by educating, integrating and shifting for good the path of Washington, D.C., strengthening our dimensional village, and my role as a Babalawo, Ifa priest and counselor, was integral in Habana Village's creation and success, however I see myself simply as an instrument of Olófin, my protector, who has all the clues and answers.

References

Author unknown (December 1, 1995). Habana Village. *The Latin Times/El Tiempo Latino*, pg 7.

Carrion, Nelly (December 1, 1995). El espíritu de "Habana Village" danza en el barrio [Habana Village's spirit dances in the neighborhood]. *Washington Hispanic*, pg 11.

www.ingramcontent.com/pod-product-compliance
Lightning Source LLC
Chambersburg PA
CBHW040249220526
45473CB00001B/424